Reminiscences...
in Silent Couplets!

Reminiscences...
in Silent Couplets!

Dipankar Das

PARTRIDGE
A Penguin Random House Company

To order additional copies of this book, contact
Partridge India
000 800 10062 62
orders.india@partridgepublishing.com

www.partridgepublishing.com/india

Contents

Prologue

"Reminiscences...in silent couplets" is a journey which I started on 8th January, 2012 and this trip continued for next one and half years.

Rhyming couplets are often used in early modern English poems and they are one of the simplest rhyme schemes in poetry.

These couplets sought to be understood in heart and soul with the sight of nature that shaped the feelings, lives, places, moments, seasons and many, in composition to give a dream into reality.

Enjoy and peruse... these rhymes of my small
creative passage with nature's melody...

-dd.
Guwahati, India/August 15, 2014

Acknowledgements

In this short voyage, I offer my prayer to God and the
Institutions that shaped me; salutation to my father and mother;
thankful to Siddhartha, Nirmali, Aniruddha, Anirban and
countless near and dear one for their love and care.

My gratitude to Dr. Harsha Bhattacharjee, Dr. Jyotirmay
Biswas, Dr. Panna Deka, Dr. Kalyan Das, Dr. Pankaj, Apurba
and Rajashree for their constant encouragement.

Many thanks to Bhaskar Saikia for his assistance in designing the work.

Special thanks to entire team of Partridge Publishing India.

And also thankful to silent cheers of someone who was the
source of my inspiration in this piece of creative effort…

Ekalavya...

Ekalavya touched the pinnacle of learning...
Sought to find out dexterity in archery,
Rejected by his teacher to illuminate,
Took the challenge and resolved with more keenness,
In the silent moonlight, he pierced the bull's eye, myriad;
Even better than Acharya's first disciple,
Ekalavya, all alone, opened the door of self learning;
From the shapeless, guideless and emptiness,
He roused...
Still to give the supreme sacrifice of his learning,
Throwing away, his cut off thumb;
And laid down the example of unconditional commitment,
Ekalavya touched the pinnacle of learning!

My Search...

I wondered what my pen spoke...
In the subtle spirit pouring out many languages,
Intellect often tuned with the expressive feeling,
Thousand strokes of brush often searched for the divine creation.

Thoughts that came out from the mind and soul,
Beauty and its realization surfaced quite often, in time;
Reality of truth was seen in the wandering eyes of a child of the blind king,
Words became luminous; thoughts became nature's music,
And my search for realization went on and on!

Unfolding the nature's prettiness stroked so much diversity,
Angels with their crown stars, made me wakeful,
Seven Gods sat there in loom of bliss...
Walked slowly in the conscious mind of golden paradise,
And my exploration for new Eden was no more!

Nectar Lake

Thought of deep inclusion in the nature,
And thinking of God in the oceanic immorality,
Nectar Lake - for all!

When, we, as a lamp in windless place;
Mind and body seemed absolutely under control,
With unification of the self with Him...

Soul of existence, hidden in the body,
Churning the ocean, self was cleansed,
Oh pure soul! Let the master of chariot cross the unscathed ocean...

Eternal India I

Blessed my country in immortal testimony,
The glorious contour of our ancient civilization,
And its fame has spread to every land,
The limitless glory surrounds...

Of all great deeds of infinite power, She is here;
To overcome the evils and always to face the change,
The enormous power of my nation,
The ever divine-India! My India!

The day shall arise to the universal hymn of the world,
The strength and power in divine touch,
The tri-colour flies up,
Bounding infinite energy of a sacred Sun,

The days have come to insight,
And fight the existing shortcomings,
Make the immortal existence more glorious,
To uplift more by eternal infinite, impending power!

Joy of sky......

When I gazed onto the sky,
The stars looked upon me,
Gleaming with infinite delight,
The stars, poetry of heavenly wanderers!

Joy of star watching in the silent sky,
Different assemblage glowing like trinkets of bliss,
Eternal light sparked by the moving asteroids,
Made the sky glow in the spring night.

The stars excelled like a living song,
With all admonishing appeal,
Many of them taught us and smiled,
Shinning up in the night sky!

The New Year call!

The day after night mizzle... sky reminded me of mid- April;
New- year, the maiden day embraced the occasion;
And drums, in the far, echoed the sounds;
And the beautiful flowers in the garden bloomed...

The day gazed just about,
Petals looked fresh and flew freely in the open air,
Blue bird, flying in the morning sky;
And the garden smiled in different greeting moods.

Tulip and sprout showed its grace,
Some blossomed and other fell and even lost,
But when they smiled,
Each one made the garden... coloured,
O nature! This was the youthful primetime of the spring...

In my wings...

In my wings,
Many feathers stroked and I flew...
Over the small oasis in the turbulent wind,
Taking to the sky, directionless,
Dipping into so many difficult junctures.
In another incredible journey!
Life formed in dancing rain,
Running away to another shiny day,
Cold arid region made my voyage often difficult,
Even, I could not take rest for a moment,
Hovering, soaring up and down,
Overcoming my obstacles, I flew...

I sat my voyage,
Propelling the clouds,
Charmed by wild blue beauty,
And enjoyed the sky of splendour...

I could do nothing but to stay on,
Going through the moment of delight in the mid air,
My ride with its way,
Flying high and high...

Clouds and my soul...

Clouds moved on,
The moon, stars and all were in the close shade,
Majesty sky,
Encircled my wings, playfully!
The full moon with cerise rays,
Lighted up so many souls,
Each night, life moved to the next,
Forever... towards the eternity!
Buddha, in each and every being,
Trying to make the soul in perfection,
The sage within us taught...
The upright path and for shunning many of the unwanted ones,
Quest of the life, demanded scores of...
Nirvana then came in life's flame!

The moonlit tonight gleamed at the fullest,
Sighted between the shades of leaves,
And moonshine from the megalomoon,
Engender million smiles...

To Him...

The giver of all knowledge and devotion,
Of bliss, salvation & pure intellect,
I bowed down to You in profound admiration!

Thousand emissions stirred in mind,
And I remained wordless...
Art though surfaced manifold in the form of anonymity,
Often, in the sphere of inseparable.

The light of divine,
Raised away from the perception,
And created amazing laceworks of thoughts,
He had become all, the eternal seer,
Divine communion unfolded...

Monsoon Rain

The clouds consigned their treasure,
Drops from the heaven refreshed the summer,
Wetted the thirsty ground many times;
Heart-beats of the men in field were opened up,
With unbound joy, some dwelled in its shower,
The monsoon rain...

Out of window, pool of drops seemed perched,
Some, cragged around the bamboo roof,
Every moment, it brought the shade of rainbow,
In the distant, clear, after-rained sky,
Hung on shower, arch of many lights coloured by moist glare,
And the evening beam of smile again,
Made after the beautiful sprinkling,
The Monsoon rain...

The nature I lived in,
With million dreams in my mind,
I sailed a 'Silver boat',
And preferred to wander in solitude....
Sudden breeze of celestial experience,
Drops in the waterfall,
And the flowing water passed through,
In continual union, with the sea,
My reminiscence awaked in the stream of flow...

O blissful astute,
Thou sculpture, the identity of all,
The perpetual, and inspired all cause,
Beyond the edge of nature,
Art accord unending,
Ahead of all obscurity...

Thou sky and high...

In natures' art and form,
Even in the whirlpool,
Moment absorbed and passed,
Innumerable cloud bursts,
Generated the tempest in mind,
Moving on-course and saluting...
The all pervading soul, in harmony!

A score of existence of a tree faced the sky,
And a lot, men of music rode with joy,
We raced, when the fortitude flew high,
And paced others in verse so, side by side.
What felt from the heart, expressed in rhythm;
With life for never being old, yet new every moment,
The tree, on the journey, was still high in the air,
Brisk cloud and raindrops...
Down to us, near and more close by!

Eternal India II

Proud moment for all of us yet again,
Our republic...
The shinning splendour Rajpath,
Carrying the destiny of the largest democracy of the world,
We looked up with all admiration and respect,
The ever flying tricolour...

The glory of sacrifice,
Honoured with reverse rifle and battle helmet,
In Amar Jawan Jyoti,
Memorial of immortal soldiers,
Echoing the 'Vandemataram'!

My country with all glory,
In the silence that echoed thousand words,
My Nation...Pride of all Indians,
In purity, sacrifice and bravery;
I bow thee, O! Motherland...

Another Beautiful Calendar Day...

Enchanting beauty of the morning sun,
Fresh, jolly and bright,
Tender picture of lovely sunlight hours,
Made the gentle breeze,
It's grace...

Many tulips in the paradise,
Singing aloud in a choir,
Gentle wind on the overflowing river,
Tapping with time...

Harmonious sweet voice there,
Resembling more like an unforgettable poetry,
The day woke up for a second time.
In the beauty and each day very divine and pure,
Sun pouring down its happiness on us,
On another beautiful calendar day!

God's particle...

My conscious inference from untouched perception,
Was it science, fiction or both?
Might be the widest dream in the history,
When vacuum was scooped out,
Dream and then in reality which sorted the imagination,
In our mind, into the larger science,
One's own place with a standing,
God, even saw His particle with an answer,
And time and again larger query waited!

Scattering particles...
Some Bosons, some Fermions;
When the half integral spin made the building block,
Photon passed its phase into a novice Boson,
And became the fundamental binding force,
Gluing around the ever expanding Universe,
Alpha particle in existence, spanned on its rotation,
The super symmetric phenomenon in astral!

In spiral,
Passed billion light years,
Dark matters in cosmic system,
Made the super massive creation of starburst,
The milky way in the deep sky,
Ignited the fiery exhalation;
In many fixed stars, born the chain;
Evolving rotund stars, small and big;
Making the abstruse galaxies, in flash!

Sun Temple

The majestic splendour, the Sun temple...
Samba got his curse,
Good lord cured him as His blessings,
And the temple shined even in the dark night...

I heard the serene message of the dawn,
Behold the morning mist,
Soul of life merged in the trance,
All reality of our true existence,
Every bit of heart harmonized,
In all nature,
When in the moments of solitude,
Moved with time and space...

The chariot with the crowning glory,
Radiating spokes on it, made it grander,
Moved over the time in all brilliance,
Sun temple, the masterpiece and majestic symbol,
Embraced high!

Take up the Radiance...

Ignorance was mere privation,
Consciousness sat down motionless,
Statue unborned often,
Wisdom gone in the age and time,
Eternity in prejudice.

If thou knew, not thyself;
Bystander sighted in all silence,
To witness the ongoing time,
Ignorance reigned as headless itself.
A vile in mind's eye and feelings,
Right way took up the radiance...
For the better human race!

Creation of waves in mind,
Soul reflected,
The sight, hidden stimulated,
In many unconcealed change in time and space,
Lighted lamp in the 'third eye',
Illuminated one and the nature,
Mind higher than high and imperishable,
In breath, and all sense appendages,
Meditating in all, in solitary place,
In infinite spirit, this was one in all,
Ignorance shattered by the true gen,
Revealed the absolute,
In achiever, enjoyer and knower!
Non duality...to triumph over!

My India...

Land of pilgrimage...
My India!
Multidimensional in reality,
The focus of maiden hour...
The 15th August, another novel day!
To unite all,
Faith in One's self, in all integration,
The torchbearer, raising themselves,
And their conviction of the power of goodness,
To elevate all without injuring the core,
In the greater India, this new INDIA!

Eternal Bliss...

Reminiscence filled my mind...
Past in cloak-hour engrossed,
Memories of yester-years,
Applauded my inner world!

The night and the shinning moon...
Departs Spartan–like,
Among the million stars, setting the horizon,
Sparkling in the cosmic sky,
Night murkiness awakes,
The moonshine comes down onto us,
Eternal bliss surrounds...

Painting reflected on...
Begun mere metaphors,
Crossing the ocean of imagination,
As the portrayal had done the best,
Recollections invigorated.
Lot music sent unto...
Here, gone another day,
A murmur from the silent image,
Refreshed the drifting mood.
When I searched for tiny fern,
Bloomed galore in the garden,
Falling leaves and petals,
Remained fresh in the nature.

Innumerable anther and stigma,
Trapped attention of the astute eyes,
Lots of parallel venation of the falling leaves,
Along other unblossomed buds,
Showered in the rain, the changing season.

Sprouting from small twig of life,
Bloomed, withered and dropped,
Beauty remained ever!

Lap of nature...

In the lap of nature,
Mature flower sprouted,
Near end of the mounting stylus,
Spores and megaspores,
All enjoyed the moment,
The fruit, all awaits,
The journey of life flourished....

Foot prints on the shore,
Started moving away with a gush of rivulet,
As I travelled on and on,
From phase to phase,
While the shore of ocean again cleaned-up,
To make a room for a caravan steps,
Starry eyes in the moonlight, in cheerful flash,
In many half dreamt mind and eyes,
Showed the destiny and fruit,
Bloomed, shined and waned...

Further I explored...
In many nameless consort,
With a lighting lamp in the heart,
Coaxing the inner feelings,
Scores of pledge for the future, to craft;
And my voyage for more nectar filled life carried on...

Vacant handcart...

Nature in the backdrop,
Visible garment of creation,
Reflections of many hidden beauties,
With collective appeal...

Often nature thrilled the eyes,
Attracted so many souls,
And thousand smiles evolved,
In all purity...

Piece of music of the nature, again...
With many answers for the living souls!

A lone vacant handcart,
In the deserted village,
Scorched in the broad daylight,
Outside the realm's courtyard...

I spent the long moment,
Sitting quietly, all alone,
Down the bank of the stream,
Someone peeped in my early morning reverie,
Emerged as an angel from the wonderland!

The clamour from the sky...

Reverberation of old gold songs,
Stories of splendid uniqueness voiced,
In days of struggle,
Resonate in more reawakened tune...

Of many stars of the sphere,
Captured the treasure,
And the power will conquer thee in the battle, by virtue,
Of thine own might!

The clamour from the sky.
Sea and land, down in the sphere,
Floating white clouds, I travelled on and on,
The moment over the earth and air, I sought after.

Discerning eyes for the bystander,
Sight of the gorgeous globe at large,
The moment lived in our eyes and heart,
Howsoever long we strived.

Nature's beauty from up the sky,
Looking to the remote scope in charming grace,
And I moved a little with every running tide...

The drops of rain

The morning, the partly cloudy and showery day;
Drops of rain knocking the pane, broke the absorption of silence,
Clouds seemed hover over, again and again;
The tune of some distant song hummed in the ears, in low pitch;

I imagined a face in the curving clouds,
Waiting for the blue sky to return,
In many nets of my heart,
Great bonds filled, often;
With endless ecstasy!

Did you hear the same music in aloofness?
Sitting in your world...
Melody, making me... eternally anew, again!

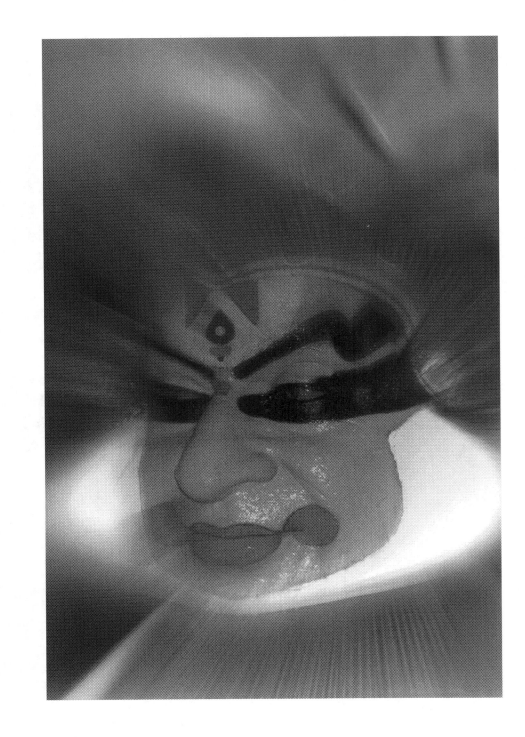

Unmasking...

Man in many camouflages,
Unmasking the disposition,
Shaman like earth-tree,
String with deep roots in the ground.

Conscious, often brute;
Bounded in nature,
Bold, free and fearless,
Superman in all folds,
Having good and awful make-up,
Made in steel, clay and wax,
Hero for others,
Dwelling in the wild streets,
Older he nurtured,
And someone adored him for his character and mind,
A life of a man...

Ever fresh appearance,
With a hidden inner prose,
Mixing the tune of nature,
Roved the feeling...

Muse came to life,
In boundless forms of shade,
God of little creation again evoked the life,
And echoed the waves in the soul and mind!

Magic Orchard...

Wide orchard of season reflected,
Garden gave much more enchanted submission,
The shade of dark colour from unrivalled beauty,
Long awaited forms slashed open,
Shadow gave more colours,
Magic gleams emerged, so often;
Glimpse of the impression,
Ceaseless stars in the changing night,
Sparked the inner magnificence,
Shade of colour, brought again... the transformed spell!

Half- truth

Unborn child Abhimanyu,
In mother's womb,
Learnt the art of entering the 'Chakravyuhu',
But could not escape the exit, in reality;
The incomplete story of his father washed out in late sleepy night,
The dashing young warrior in the great battle laid down his life,
In all honour of his kinsman and lord,
The courageous character perceived,
The half-truth in mother's womb,
Before he was born,
Nature and character bloomed!

Inscape from mind...

Image inscape from mind,
Unconsciously...
Many bizarre feeling exposed at time,
Evolved out like thunderbolts,
Making my conscious wound revolt,
Reality stroked and I woke up, in reflection,
Fragments of many forms,
All in blazing strokes,
Inflamed me and my spirit, many times!

The ocean laid ideal azure in the Sun,
Beam of rays chanted the beauty,
Waves of succession made my joy uplifting,
Colourful sky made the music on the shore,
Many creepers in the breeze...
Breathe holding no more,
Drops of prettiness,
After the morning shower,
Cascade apart...
My feeling hurtled, the way I desired;
In flying high with the airstream,
Lone day escaped into the twilight,
Towards the day end,
And in the mind and psyche, unexpressed!

Goddess...

The earth within us,
And endless sky above,
The call of the cosmos,
Made our soul to respond in celestial pulsation,
Infinite power of spirit,
All worlds within Goddess...

O Mother, Thou knew all,
Remover of all distress,
Herself on the lion in the spirit of tussle,
Infinite sunshine, you brought amongst thousands of drumbeats,
With the sacred trumpet and conch.

Goddess with the family, invoked in the mother earth,
To save us, purify us,
To win over the wickedness,
With bursting strength and You came racing onward,
O Mother, O Durga,
Let your triumph be everywhere, every corner of earth!

When we submit ourselves thy behest,
In many overt forms, many names,
Holy hymn keeps us awake,
Mother in her all light, spread out...
The waves of bliss often walloped us,
In shapeless transmigration,
Whilst Goddess touched each soul...

Her image blossomed in our half closed eyes,
Song of Her praise evident again and again.
Divine promise in all purification,
Even in one's solitude,
Thy knew all!

The day of prayer ended,
Thousand light in every corner,
Mingled with smoke...
Metrical intonation rose at time,
Hovering the deity in their eyes,
The fragrance of setting sun's rays,
Filled our heart, ever joyfully!

Journey in my dream

Journey in my dream...
In many abstraction of unknown grace,
Followed the steps in space and time,
In limitless stillness...

I walked slowly but courageously from door to door,
Witnessing the past, present and future,
Raising the soul to holy assembly,
In the kingdom of eternal voyage.

I hold the gleam of hope,
In many twirl of the sun,
Heart and soul liberated,
In nameless divine.

I longed for the realisation,
Many recalls fade...
In my incomplete reverie!

Laid a hand on my soul...

Interfacing the nature,
In many steps in the new mystic world,
A strange listless cheerfulness,
Laid a hand on my soul,
Riding the journey in the emission of time,
Opening of the bonbon sensation,
Often, in thematic charming, at ease,
Limitless appearance manifested,
In striking expression,
And I had nothing more to say...

Morning sunrays of holy light,
A shadow of remembrances,
The song of birds from distant wood,
Raised the sleeping souls.

The triumph of the footsteps,
Surfaced from the depth,
In beautiful creations of one's life,
Memories renewed...

New time, new day.
Again tribute to the nature in a newer way,
With many folded hands...

Roving sea...

In the shore of the vast sea,
I saw the seagulls roving,
Some white and some coloured,
Charmed at its beautiful sight.

In the twilight, I stared,
And yearned that I could also fly high...

In the falling night that awaked us,
The moon seen peeping out,
Among the coloured leaves,
I thank whatever gods might be,
Thou were left all alone,
Thy spirit lived for eternal years,
In the moonlight...

Every existence would live in thee,
Come to us, the light, beautiful one;
To venture with wider imagination,
And for all this, nature came into bud...

Prayer...

O river! Thou generate the strength,
Clout can avail everything,
And the sight of Godly feelings,
So many paths of undefiled heritage flowing with,
O God! Give us the grace to accept the serenity,
Courage to overcome the change and wisdom,
Let us gallop the way it is made,
And fly like wind in the horizon,
May we speak straightway as thunder?
The steps at the distance are heard still,
And we are waiting with the belief,
That all will bring us the light,
With all enthusiasm!

Touch ...

In the fascinating sky,
With bright stars shinning up,
All have promises to keep,
And miles to move forward, before we go to sleep.

Like the sun flashing forth light,
Unto enshrouded darkness,
The greatest ascetics of the celestial bodies,
Beyond the states of waking, dream and sleep,
And we offer our salutations to that beneficent being,
The Universe which is reality, exits within herself.

Salutation to Thee,
O Lord incarnate, O lord divine,
Glory unto Thee in all His form,

Evening stars glancing in its path,
Image of 'gas giant' evolved,
And at the self that moved forward,
At distance,
Moving the pinnacle of energy with time.

When I touched upon the wild leaf,
It gave some warmth,
To find it and understand it,
And to explore it more,
In the habitation, up the hills...

Otherwise, it would have forgotten,
Its existence and beauty.
Though mistakenly, I touched her,
To weep the dust from it, freely as a cloud,
In the roadside, up the hills...

The flowers and buds in the wild,
As if were waiting for us to touch it,
The fine-looking little buds,
And its gems that treasured the nature in it!

Struggled lamp in the sky

The dark night...
Even the lamp in the sky,
Felt shy and helpless,
Shameful act never to be pardoned,
Songs of millions with watery eyed,
Will never go in vain,
But the struggling bird gone forever,
The evil shrieked, many times,
Trembled the moral sphere,
And all seemed gone to a nightmare,
Insanely...stormed the innocent!

The happening,
Scorned at all of us,
Our floating lamps in silence,
In many lonely existence,
Drifted from the shoreline,
And cruelty left... the fall of the dark night.
Gloomy sky will stare at all of us,
For the impelled justice!

Shadow of Long tunnel

I loved to watch the shadow...
At the end of the long tunnel,
When many memories lived together,
All alone.

The eyes tired enough,
And chase of light greeted the season,
Mild sunshine floated.
Where the blowing wind took me,
I flew blooming, endlessly,
And clouds were no longer anymore,
Outside my door.

The lonely wooden piece,
Floated and encouraged the voyager,
Waves rose occasionally and above,
And pleasant breeze from far, was still there...

My torn paper...

Often, in malicious banter,
Stroked the heart,
Sprint that never going to win the race,
In the erroneous discernment,
Making the will in more resolving,
When the heart and mind strapped forward,
The pen that stretched its struggling arm,
The torn paper...
Perturbed me and my virtue,
As I had a dream...too little to express,
In the closed shore of my existence,
Out of abundance of things that I possessed,
Sometime, I lost my thirst,
For little waters of life,
When I found that real sight was lost,
And my torn paper flied...

Unfurling the old stalks...

When the paddy being cut,
In that season,
Songs of plenty,
Mark the festive time,
Unfurling the old stalks,
Again they will grow,
With a fresh look...
Season changes,
Song of life changes,
Even the Sun changes its direction,
To auspicious northern turn,
And dips in the Holy Ganges remove the sin
As believed, in this spell;
But each of us needs to awake,
From the face of darkness,
And the clouds and cold will rumble away,
As the days leave behind...

Naming life...

Spreading sun in the winter,
Life that grows in all set,
A striated winged fly,
Perched her wings,
In the colour that we all see,
Shaded them in my closed palm,
For some time,
Comprising the cycle in full,
And unmaking the creation,
For the nectar...

I left myself,
Another season, cut to piece;
Garden's heart beat looked anew and fresh,
Greeting the life again and again,
And voices of many flowers,
Archived the silence,
In all purity...

My boat has to sail on,
For the incessant journey.
The waves of flow,
Moved the wooden piece,
As I am carrying the basket of flowers,
Along the lovely wooden valley,
Amid the strange unknown islands,
Resounding rivers joining the course,
In the tranquil evening.

The deep music touched the soul,
And I am finding my way,
Enjoying throughout the ride,
Listening the distant music of flute,
Echoing from the hills,
And they removed the blankness of my life!

Heritage – Golconda...

The light from the fort of Golconda,
Printed among the building blocks,
Criss- crossing the history.
Thrashed by untold stories,
Stood the time,
Of many silent conflicts,
Inhabiting every past living memories,
Along the path of colourful stones.

The evening trailed down,
All along the dark shadow,
The beaten rocks echoed,
The love tale and the drama,
Carried down the memory lanes.

The ruins raised their fountains,
In the hills, mutely,
In centuries old monuments...

In cool breeze of late evening,
Saw the nature at its best,
Ever silent,
In chase of untamed voyage.
The glories of time,
And symbol of feral power,
Lost in course… Wild at heart,
In breath-taking loveliness,
Carving the move away,
In untamed nature…

The light…
At the end of the fort's corridor,
Memories of yester-years spoken silently,
In the fistful sunrays that had stolen my sleep,
Underneath the theme, I woke-up.

The incomplete hills,
Again grew festive in the twilight,
Their splendour undiminished,
Sound, at distance, tickled the laughter,
And the vibrations echoed and hummed,
In the ruins of the fallen fort.
Reflecting the beginning,
I roamed and recollected those past times…

Illusion

Illusion...
In the turbulent depth of my mind,
When drops,
Stroked and reached the newness,
The joy scattered removing the dusts.

Illusion...
Floated from my eyes,
In the silent grace,
Wrapped like a little fresh rain.

Illusion...
I put in a colourful dream,
Among the water and clouds,
The river ripples,
Drifted far in my inner space.

Illusion...
In deep blue water from endless sky,
Danced before my weary eyes,
Many broken shinning shells,
Waked up, in the enlivening!

Someone's eye

I am charmed at someone's eye,
Trouncing down from the sky,
Soundless call outside the soul,
Fetched me the solace...

Something made me unbound,
Amity made me speechless,
Often nectar touch filed,
And sigh gushed out...

I love to witness the clouds,
And little bit of untimely drizzle,
Rain came down,
In the steps of late winter,
Making the scent of the dusts breezing out.

I am magical when I hear the sweet silent songs,
Softly...
And I will wait for the sunshine, again!

Chiasm of colours

Little breeze stroked at the sunset,
The half dried leaves, jiggled for the change,
And the gloomy sky, tossed the willow trees...

I don't see the sparrows any more, flying in the courtyard...
Remembering the days when they used to fly,
In the garden,
In and around the houses...
And the growing tall buildings,
Removed the green habitat, altogether...

I saw the artificial nests,
In the lonely desert,
Their call remained vacant,
Devoid of birds' presence...

The busy cities and spaces,
Made little one to fly somewhere else,
Distance from us...

And the green place, here;
Without the hymns of little sparrows...
With each sunrise,
With blue sky above,
Love that brought, silently;
In pure expression...

Lonely meadow intensified the tie,
O thou beautiful,
Blooming the spirit of spring arrival,
Each flower of your garland,
Made my submission!

I wonder to see the colours,
In the shade of my palm,
I close my eyes,
To keep the afterimage...

Many blue winged butterflies,
Made the move,
In the sunshine,
And they refused to be stained,
With chiasm of colours.

Oyster

A lonely song of shore-less ocean,
Drifting with the waves,
Diving down in deep and tossing,
To find the oyster...

The waves of your last touch,
Moved my outstretched hand,
Longed for the moment,
My blink gave,
Drops of silence, in many pensive moods...

Many breezes buzzing in the spring,
May colourful dreams reach you,
And fill your heart like blue eternal oyster...

Offerings...

I went to the garden,
To collect the blooming flowers,
The wreath, I made,
For the offering...

Gloomy clouds in the sky,
Made my prayers heard,
In all the bounding,
The trances often transmigrated...

The days of creation,
Passed on and on,
The night came, thereafter;
Under the shinning blue moon,
Your music at the distance,
Welcomed the unseen, every time...

The golden pearl and colour on your half body,
Floated in my imagination,
Feelings for the garland, I made;
I thought about,
The offering,
In humble submission,
The joy of infinite unfoldness,
All across the earth,
The offering...

Our life, greeted for better gifts,
Many songs flown away,
To the offering,
You belonged...

Tagore... You showed the way!

Adoration unto the lap of nature,
You Showed...
The pure messages in embodiment of existence,
In the poems of yours,
'Songs of offering',
Carried the note of infinite being,
Always free from illusion and bondage,
Bliss eternal and grace,
Thou your creations...gross and subtle,
Most sweet and equally powerful!
Many mornings awakened with sunlight,
After the light showers,
I peeped from the glassed casement,
To see the foliage at the end...

The temple bell marked the day's awakening,
Beyond the sight of dusty lanes,
On the austere, beautiful trees of early summer,
My heart too went emerald,
Amongst the abundant leaves and seasoned flowers,
Masking the cloudy time,
Through the shadowy trees,
Felt around the sight and my mind,
Something, somewhere had changed,
But not the beauty.
I felt I should stay long,
On the side of the greenery...
Beyond all darkness,
You lived...
To Thee, I bow down with my whole heart!

The Universal poet of golden age,
Million blazes were raised in the waves of ocean, time and again;
Uncountable creations touched the sphere above,
And tri nation in the globe blessed with your song of praise.

Eternity avowed your noble life,
All earth and heaven condensed into poetry,
Music from the hub of heart sent unto God,
O, thou soul of souls, poet of poets...
Generation salutes you... follow you!

Seeing the black clouds at daybreak

Often we wait for the rain to come,
Reaching us from the distant piece of black cloud,
In every touchstone and coolness.

Sat on the side of burning wood,
On the bank of flowing river,
Watching the light of image passing by,
Just at the daybreak...

Lot of deeds have to be carried on,
Many songs have to be reflected down the hills,
Before the dark night seize us and our souls,
And no one is different in that!

Raindrops will come to our doorsteps,
Teasing the weary soul,
Playfully it will wash,
The memories, grown over the past days,
In loving, caring and all struggle...

The days are passing...
As all of us have to reborn in every new day,
Till our judgement sunlight hour!

God in me...

I often think of unseen pull,
Invoked in me,
Consciously and unconsciously...

I often sensed the Mesmer's tune.
Disturbed me and my soul,
Time and again,
To gain nothing at their end,
But little God in me,
Raised its awakened hand,
Transmitted its little protection,
For the truth.
For which, I was awakened till late night;
To see the hidden reality coming out...

God in me,
Guide to ignore deceptive, unwanted things;
And to look forward for the better world...

Behold the beauty of silvery sky...

With the greening of the meadows,
By a shower of rain,
Many colours in the horizon bloomed,
Setting the jade in the bank of the hot-spring...

Behold the beauty of silvery sky,
Bubbling the dusts under,
Clearing the moving clouds, made the heaven more eloquent;
And jewel sight, appearing on the far side.

A creeper in the breeze,
And the words of nature,
Had turned my heart, more than my mind, unexpressed!
Carrying sweet smell of, after rain;
And of flora from around.

Little gentle breeze in the view-point,
Kept me fresh and awakened!

Abode of angels...

I passed the blissful night,
In the abode of angels,
The crown in me within the temple of self,
My breath deepened by unstuck sounds,
I became mute and no power to describe the feelings,
Thousand dips in the depth of unknown Ocean,
I wanted to realize how deep it was?
Running from one temple to the other...
I bowed to that radiance,
Ever peaceful and endless,
There was no space and no time, I felt;
And out of pure night that covered me,
I thanked whatever God it might be, sublimed!

Scent of Arabia

From up the sky,
Gorgeous mountains desolated,
Amazed in the reflection of sunshine,
A radiant white peaks, among the clouds;
Brought down thousand desires, as I flew over;
The space and expanse, I shifted beyond;
Be it mountains, clouds, stream, mist and then desert;
Play of nature, evoked my inner self,
And what was joy, I did not know;
God's creation and play charmed me and my eyes,
In time though!

In the Arabia,
Magnificence of land like a unique picture in mind's imagination,
Wonderful deserts and red soil hills from the horizon,
Sparked my inner emotions.

In sand-dune of the zenith,
The dream of mine from distant land, Carried the waves to the Arabian sea,
The land where first sunshine touches the Arabian earth.

Soul elated, eyes astounded,
And the dunes submerged into reality in the holy land!

Sabbath

Submerged in sands,
In many forms of waves,
Overspreading the edging land, elegantly.
The Sabbath in my lines, in loneliness;
Carrying steps in nameless dunes...an inimitable feeling of mine, though!

Perplexing the sights,
Treasure trove of Arabia,
Like a splendid solstice.

Our meeting into unison,
The footsteps of the cavalcade,
And symphony of Bedouin's melodic music,
And the mirage is still there...

What would mean for me?
Uninhabited track of sands made of sharp curves,
All alone under the blue sky,
The secret of legitimacy in the bliss...

Footsteps in the wild journey,
As I moved in the oasis,
The lonely desert plant looked at me,
And flower in it, smiled.

Gentle wind from the distant sea blew,
Pleasing the diligent camel safari,
The life that was always simple and immaculate,
At the courtyard of conception!

Rhymes in caves

I walked day long,
The twilight already ahead of time,
In the caves of mountains,
The breeze of blowing winds on the shore,
Amongst the background sun...

In the journey of transitory life,
Many shades of breath taking moments,
Stood between me and thy veracity,
Beautiful day break from the east, evoked my soul, next day.

My prayer for the utmost valour,
Thousand steps to surmount,
Prayers of faith called me and my soul,
In the sandy land.

In the world, Oh! God!
I searched for the eternal call,
Faith of all gave my prayer, all stateliness;
In the beautiful day of sunrise
When the first light was dazzling.

Again, same rhythm will be repeated, on and on;
The time and moment will fly,
Only the imprint of moments will remain,
In sands, rocks and the foot hills,
Gorgeous caves bade the farewell,
With the sunset!

Mirage

I looked at the distance,
In the sunlit sandy boulevard,
Found the mirage moving away from us,
As we move onward...

There was no way of catching the illusion,
In the shiny water surface,
And its shadow of reflected desert trees,
Made it more pragmatic.

The mirage was just a day dream,
And my thirst increased,
And tired chase was somewhat in vain,
In sandy reflected alleyway,
At the distance...

Mirage had many inquiries,
In mind and sight,
Something, from nowhere in the far land,
Showed the hope,
Even though it may not be real,
But the fantasy was still far...

Land of Frankincense

When there is no beginning and thus, no end;
In the endless span of moments,
We embraced our imagination,
Beyond our measly subsistence...

Facets of never ending beauty,
Raised the spirit of us,
We wished to explore many,
In all eternity...

When shades of leaves,
Taking new colours,
The winds are making number of thumps,
A stranger from far distance,
Waked us in early daybreak.

We expressed our delight,
In the magic land,
Each day we had fallen,
And then enjoyed again.

As we had the foundation,
Of joy of warm smile,
Our world became one,
In blissful season!
Natural magnetism of nearby mountains,
Frankincense trees welcome one and all in the land.

In the south of Arabian land,
When you see at the distance,
Coconut trees and sewn boats,
The evergreen lush and green of terrain,
A land of monsoon,
In the desert land.

Baobab foliage makes the ceaseless call,
In beautiful beaches and coastline,
String up the beautiful inner feelings,
In the land of antiquity!

It boasts of ruins and fortified towns,
Reminds of ancient civilization,
The land where mountains meet the sea,
Numerous make shift field where young boys,
Roll their magical feats with football,
A land of Frankincense, Salalah- A souvenir of Oman!

Bridge of shades in Arabia

I sat on the rock edge,
Beside vast sea,
With every change of place, I enjoyed;
And felt wholesome...

Many sizzling change of my sit out,
Cleaved the aroma,
And in the twilight,
Among chirping sounds of my fellow birds,
I set for departure...
The trees shed their leaves,
Changed the colour from greenery to yellow,
And paved the way, my precedent.

Whiff of ever fresh air,
Swarmed my feelings under the blue sky,
And I will return to my nest, again!

Passage of my travel,
In dreams of my journey,
Shinned in between the rays,
Long sunny days,
In the winter season peeped,
In celebration of life...

Sunway made the glow,
In the floating air,
Delicate winds from nowhere,
Bridged the shades,
As I moved on and on!

Dreams in mind's eye

I am an amateur dreamer,
Dreamt of great nebula,
High-up in the horizon,
In spiral, loops and whirlpools.

I came out with great design,
In my little microscopic world,
Finding few attractive dusts almost similar,
Budging out the old and new stars.

Form crystallized into the passion,
Creator gave the colour,
Man's enchantment expressed diverse,
From union of dream and realism.

Precision counted on and on,
Nature belled the true gist,
In accepting the spirit and theme,
Magnum opus spoke for itself...

I am an amateur dreamer,
Came out in concert
Envisaging many billion galaxies,
Sometime, Magellanic Clouds covered my sight,
Dreamer like me, mapping imagination in mind's eye!

Joy of ecstatic colours

In the daylight of life,
Little ray of colour sparkle;
After a shower of rain,
Sun herald again, with delight...

Elated colours of beautiful rainbow,
Touched the aroma of life,
True beauties of colour never hide,
And effect reckons the season as it is passing by...

With a new day, my thoughts breezed out;
In attractive imagination of life,
Enjoying the lesser things that I knew,
And admiring the beauty to know with difference.

What I do thinking about the tempest?
Trying to sail my boat in the spirit,
In long journey, sometime wing shakes my boat;
Life is like all about.

Nature turns round about,
The exquisiteness comes to the extension,
Existing in the very flare,
All multipart into one.

The quick look of eternity,
Again to go unapproachable afar!
Magic charm needs new bud in the spring,
Bathe away few past with modest shower;
Life moves on with ample shades,
Beauty and colour sees what no eyes see...

Moving cosmos

Cosmos is ever on the move,
Thought in being are ever changing,
Dreams and reveries that never same always,
One move forward with lighted torch…

My search for glowing and radiance meteor shower,
Recall the rifts among the falling stars,
Each small stars making the fireball,
In decoration at the acme of the Milky Way…

The self, like dark clouds in the blue,
Even the Sun cannot be seen through;
As drizzle clears the black clouds,
So, sinking the ego, one is free and better...

Man, able to attain the highest;
Often accrue the power in silence,
After the day of austerity, truth is comprehended,
All else is delusion!

Unknown ray of existence in the vast cosmos,
In speedy motion, dole out of the light
And foretell the life beyond...

Titanic lost,

100 years after, 10th of April, 2012

Dark clouds and unseen iceberg on that fateful day,
"Titanic lost" in the heart of Atlantic, marked 100 years;
The day was very last for those, today…100
years back, when it started it's trip;
And voyage of mere five days was last for those,
Who never returned again…

The journey showed the character of unbound courage,
When musician ran their fingers on strings, till the last moment;
The heroic captain rouses to the occasion to see the final destiny,
And the last kiss of romance iced up forever,
The great titanic went down…and it was all over,
On that awful night!

Big Bang…

Big bang…
Reality came about billion years back,
Infinite stars, then born and created;
Life spawned thou…

Journey of stars moved the course silently,
Many disappeared in black hole,
Existence found in response,
Life spawned thou…

Countless galaxies sang the tune,
Survival of theme marched forward,
Soul of Universe lifted the progression,
Life spawned thou…

Thou celestial rays pour in,
Primeval power excites in many,
Million liveliness refuse in all make-up
O Eternal one, Thou art creates and maintains the little evergreen nature,
Often absolute silence uplift the Universe in cosmic form,
Life spawned thou…

Conch shell...

Inside the twisted conch shell,
Once, life saw its existence,
Drops of sea water rolled in many times,
The beauty created now and life had gone out of it,
Blooming in its purest form,
Conch left to blow in the clarion calls…

Coral shined marked its attractiveness,
In little appearance of tenderness,
Looking divine with its character,
Gorgeous from within and without,
Life and beauty yearned for sublime,
And drew the mind with a caring power,
Shining through its crystalline casing,
Spring so many heart and soul!

Life in conch offered loveliness in the world,
Looked anew made it much richer,
Even empty shell spoke,
And I realized that life had gone out of the shell,
Still making a glow at its best, for us!

Soul of existence

Soul of existence.
Dangle aloft by its splendour,
Waft of past, slipping down the memory lane;
Shinning like a moonlight smile...

Sometime pleasure, sometime grief;
Rolling many things in life to forget;
Gust of feeling wipes our whinge,
Parting the dark, a new day emerge...

Life is like pearl,
Made everything gorgeous than it could be,
The clarion call evoked me in this shiny day,
To sail this boat of life smoothly...

Celebration is still on,
In the soul and mind,
Song of bird from close by hedging bush,
Remind us the season and the merry time...

Butterfly effect and time image

Butterfly moves away from my grasp,
When I intend to hold her,
She alights upon me, happily;
When I am in silent and in tranquil.

Likewise, I chased the happiness,
And it flew away from my reach,
Joy tried to revolve around me,
When I am indifferent.

Time image and it shadow,
Running fast forward…
Every count makes a history,
And moment passed, it is lost forever.

Evolve the time in reflection,
Past, present and future in our clock face,
Vibrant contour keep us awake,
Oh time! Show your image!

Whirlpool tides

All day, in our boat, we sailed;
And found ourselves amongst you all,
Keeping the balance in between the whirlpool tides.

Many times we moved,
In the shadow of bamboo clumps,
And reading the water of shallow river,
Niche in rocks near bank and untamed breeze.

Peaks of winter hills by the side of river,
Down the valley, all scenic beauty reflected,
Cold breeze flowed then,
In memory, lushness remained.

Swaying in the wild wind,
We sailed in trivial water and smiled,
Seeing you, today, having a cherry time;
Come on, our friend, once again!

Recall and Feral nature

Old man brought to mind his precedent,
The golden moments of his early life,
Playing the melody of his care free days,
His juncture, we all will go by...

Thou in nature,
Enlightening the beauty in mind,
Stream of thoughts outrivaled the orb,
Calm in nearby descended....

Lovely beehives in trees,
Stood tall,
Forest primeval in lonely existence,
Replicated the old man's pride again...

Smoke filled his pipe,
Reminiscence faded in the jungle twilight,
Some cared for him, other ignored,
Smoke in his pipe died out...

Soaring Kites

Soaring kites in the cove of setting sun,
They loved and took part in the course,
Acts came to display from crypt of twine,
With soft closed murmur, they flew again…

Days, seasons and yearns flying by,
Instant love for each other in the strongest chase,
Never their voyage was self-possessed in the wind,
Cord could not hold them under duress any more.

Search for life in the twilight hour,
Lived more in unknown attraction,
They glanced with the wind,
Elegance of their presence resided in thee.

Their nature guided by bond of strings,
Nearness graced their limit,
Love for each other in single recreation,
And with the sunset, the romance ended for the time being!

Awake my mind... Awake

Awake my mind, gentle awake,
When I see the pure white swan,
Pray my life, to be simple and straight,
At the concourse of creation and beauty...

Mind illusion...real or unreal,
One tunes and impression...appears like thought,
Imagined in all creating sense,
Wherever someone covered the mind and sight,
It's all truth, escaped from the shade.

Tears speak more than heart, echoes the inner feeling;
Smile becomes bright with tears upon,
Sparkle the effect and often rain-bowed out;
Drops of pearl can humanise the soul...

Imagination of creation has beautiful notion,
As footprints in mind's sand dune,
Gathered all the day till the dusk,
Little dust from the soften rocks, made;
The charming music of our life,
Awake my mind, gentle awake!

Ripples in life

Ripples, little mystery in life,
Sublime in it's being,
Creates so many chores on its way;
Live harmoniously in the waves of life.

The zenith opens its awning of indigo,
Imaginations build up in solitude,
When thought saw the beauty,
Forms become divine.

Beautiful ripples…
Big and small,
Shower rejoice the moment,
Gracious drops creates the waves,
And dazzling undulations,
Smiling in the flowing breeze…

Raindrops--A nature's melody

Beautiful raindrops, boost of nature;
Recollect the sweet music of mind,
And I hear the sound of delightful morning rain,
Drops striking the windowpane.

Dimple pool over the bud, ever appealing;
Playing the soft pleasurable nature's melody,
Passing the moment under flying shadowy clouds,
And raindrops refreshed the nature, again and again!

Rain drops make me in high spirit,
Thousand thunders in cloudy sky,
And rain washes the earth,
Dusty whiff and water dancing everywhere.

Rain means for the season and the harvest,
Till the ripe occasion,
From deep silence of the field,
And to joyous rhythm of all seasons.

The fresh clean air then touches us,
Sun glowing again out of blue sky,
With million smiles, get in touch with,
And bright rays refreshed everyone, once again!

Dew drops

Morning dew drops…
On the heart of leaves and smiling flowers,
Nature's tear shed,
To come out of celestial happiness,
Morning dew drops…

Season's leaves clenched stronger,
After the night, in early morning;
And silent dews hovering at its best;
In nature's heaven…

Twinkling over the scorching leaves,
Follow many beauties,
Dew drops…you are just there, after all!

I always knew you

I felt that I always knew you,
Beyond touch…
Beyond words…

So much known,
Many unknown that flew between us,
Limitless…

Beautiful songs,
Blissful rhythm in air,
Nature bloomed with us, in every step;
In the chase of thrilling strings.

Spreading loveliness,
In time, when we met;
And it was heavenly occurrence,
In the mind's vintage shoreline…

Pure at heart and deed,
In all silent togetherness.
When I felt, I always knew you…
Beyond touch, beyond words!

Songs of life taught me

When I tried to see the world,
With the stroke of my realization,
Many songs of yester years taught me,
Time to time, how to sing?

Something healed out of it,
Some showed the real path,
In the journey of difficult terrain.

I, often lost within hour's darkness,
I lost what's mine,
The shadow of someone,
Reborn in me,
And swept my inner feeling away…